T0198803

THE 12 DISCIPLES OF JESUS

BOOK TWO

WRITTEN BY
TEMALESI W.M.K. SAVOU

ILLUSTRATED BY
BETHANY WHITWELL

ISBN: Softcover   978-1-5434-0327-5
        EBook   978-1-5434-0326-8

Print information available on the last page

Rev. date: 08/25/2017

To order additional copies of this book, contact:
Xlibris
1-800-455-039
www.xlibris.com.au
Orders@Xlibris.com.au

PHILIP

This is Philip.

Philip was born in a fishing village called Bethsaida, near the sea of Galilee.

Philip has a sister, her name is Mariamne.

Philip lives with his sister and his family in a big house near the sea.

SEA OF GALILEE

WELCOME TO BETHSAIDA

One day, a very kind and humble looking man came to his village.

His name was Jesus.

Philip did not know Jesus,
but Jesus knew him.

Jesus saw Philip in the village and told Philip to follow him.

Philip left his house, the village, his family and everything to follow Jesus.

Philip became one of Jesus's disciple.

NATHANAEL

This is Bartholomew, he is also called
Nathanael which means "God has given."

Bartholomew was born in Cana in Galilee, outside of Jerusalem.

He is an Israelite.

This is Bartholomew's dad.
His dad is a farmer.

His dad named him Bartholomew
because he is a son of a farmer.

They have a big fig tree outside their house and Bartholomew loves to sit under the fig tree during the day.

Bartholomew has a friend named Philip who enjoys to sit with him under the fig tree.

Philip said, "we have found the one Moses wrote about in the law, And about whom the prophets also wrote. Jesus of Nazareth, the son of Joseph".

"Nazareth! Can anything good come from there?" Bartholomew asked.

"Come and see", said Philip.

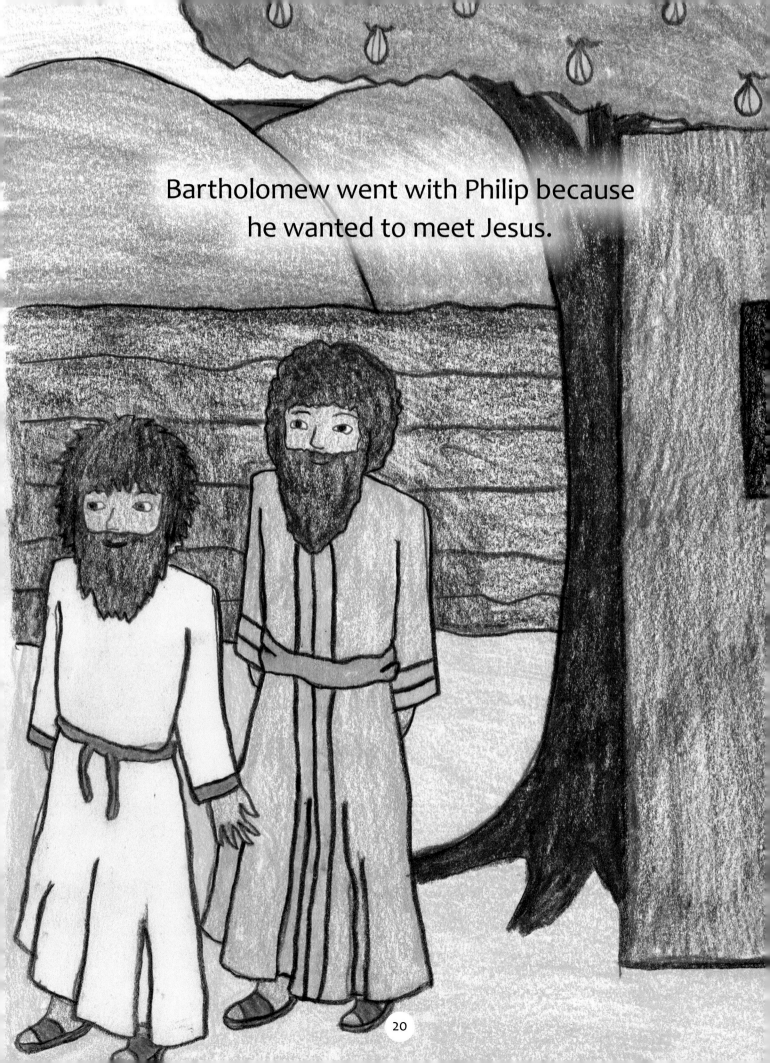

Bartholomew went with Philip because
he wanted to meet Jesus.

When Bartholomew met Jesus, Jesus told him that he saw him while he was still under the fig tree before Philip called him.

Bartholomew was amazed and believed Jesus on that day. He left everything and followed him.

He became the 6th disciple of Jesus.

THOMAS

My name is Thomas, I am one of Jesus' disciples.

24

I was born in Galilee, a city near the sea called the Sea of Galilee.

My family and friends call me "Judas the Twin" because I have a twin brother.

I am a Jew.

I go to the temple every Sabbath to pray. This is the Temple, it is also called the Synagogue.

One day we heard that Jesus' friend, Lazarus had died because he was very sick.

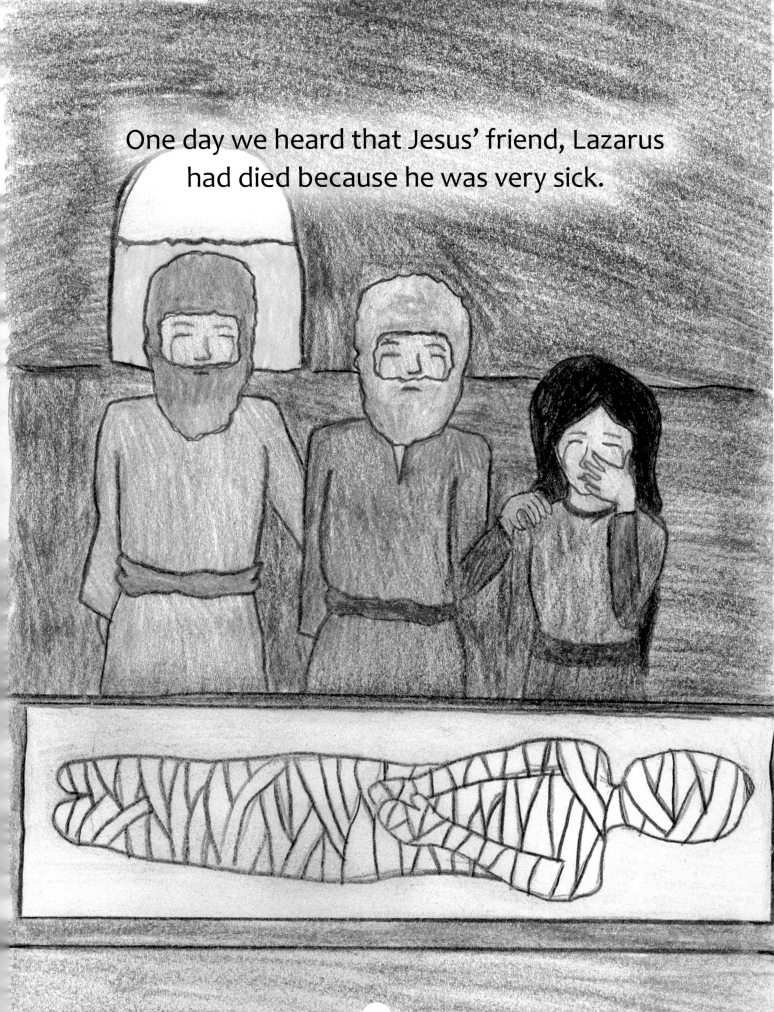

Jesus said to us, "let us go back to Judea".
Jesus wanted us to see Lazarus his friend.

JUDEA

Some of the disciples were afraid because the people were trying to kill Jesus. I was not afraid, "Let us also go; that we may die with him", I told the disciples.

Then the rest of the Disciples and I went with Jesus to Bethany. We witnessed Jesus raising Lazarus from the Dead.

No one tried to kill Jesus on that day,

I was willing to die with Jesus.

MATTHEW

This is Levi. He is also called Matthew.

Matthew lived in Capernaum. It is a fishing village near the shore of the sea of Galilee.

Matthew was taught how to read and count. But he loves counting more than reading.

Matthew became a Publican when he grew up. He became a very important man in the Roman government.

Matthew collects money from the people which belongs to the government. It is called Tax.

People called Matthew the 'Tax Collector'.

People would come to Jerusalem
to pay their taxes to Matthew.

WELCOME
TO
JERUSALEM

People believed that Matthew would keep half of the money he collects from the people and he would give half to the government. Matthew became a very rich man.

One day as Jesus was visiting Jerusalem he walked pass Matthew's office in the city,

he saw Matthew sitting on his table collecting tax from the people.

"Follow Me", Jesus said to him.

43

Immediately Matthew got up, left everything and followed Jesus.

Matthew became one of Jesus' 12 disciples.

In the next book, we shall read about
the last four disciples of Jesus.

Printed in the United States
By Bookmasters